JAPANESE DINNER COOKBOOK

A JAPANESE COOKBOOK FILLED WITH EASY JAPANESE RECIPES FOR SIMPLE JAPANESE COOKING

By
BookSumo Press

Published by
BookSumo Press,
http://www.booksumo.com/

ABOUT THE AUTHOR.

BookSumo Press is a publisher of unique, easy, and healthy cookbooks.

Our cookbooks span all topics and all subjects. If you want a deep dive into the possibilities of cooking with any type of ingredient. Then BookSumo Press is your go to place for robust yet simple and delicious cookbooks and recipes. Whether you are looking for great tasting pressure cooker recipes or authentic ethic and cultural food. BookSumo Press has a delicious and easy cookbook for you.

With simple ingredients, and even simpler step-by-step instructions BookSumo cookbooks get everyone in the kitchen chefing delicious meals.

BookSumo is an independent publisher of books operating in the beautiful Garden State (NJ) and our team of chefs and kitchen experts are here to teach, eat, and be merry!

INTRODUCTION

Welcome to *The Effortless Chef Series*! Thank you for taking the time to purchase this cookbook.

Come take a journey into the delights of easy cooking. The point of this cookbook and all BookSumo Press cookbooks is to exemplify the effortless nature of cooking simply.

In this book we focus on Japanese cooking. You will find that even though the recipes are simple, the taste of the dishes are quite amazing.

So will you take an adventure in simple cooking? If the answer is yes please consult the table of contents to find the dishes you are most interested in.

Once you are ready, jump right in and start cooking.

— BookSumo Press

TABLE OF CONTENTS

Any Issues? Contact Us

If you find that something important to you is missing from this book please contact us at info@booksumo.com.

We will take your concerns into consideration when the 2nd edition of this book is published. And we will keep you updated!

— BookSumo Press

LEGAL NOTES

COMMON ABBREVIATIONS

cup(s)	C.
tablespoon	tbsp
teaspoon	tsp
ounce	oz.
pound	lb

*All units used are standard American measurements

Chapter 1: Easy Japanese Recipes

Glazed Japanese Chicken Wings

Ingredients

- 3 lb chicken wings
- 1 egg, lightly beaten
- 1 C. all-purpose flour for coating
- 1 C. butter
- SAUCE
- 3 tbsp soy sauce
- 3 tbsp water
- 1 C. white sugar
- 1/2 C. white vinegar
- 1/2 tsp garlic powder, or to taste
- 1 tsp salt

Directions

- Before you do anything preheat the oven to 350 F.
- Slice the wings into half and coat them with the beaten egg. Dust the wings in the flour.
- Place a large frying pan over medium heat. Heat the oil in it. Add the chicken wings and cook them until they become deep golden brown.
- Drain the chicken wings and place them in a roasting dish.
- Get a mixing bowl: Mix in it the remaining ingredients. Pour the mix all over the wings and toss them to coat.
- Cook the chicken wings in the oven for 38 min. Serve them warm.
- Enjoy.

Amount per serving (6 total)

Timing Information:

Preparation	15 m
Cooking	45 m
Total Time	1 h

Nutritional Information:

Calories	675 kcal
Fat	44.3 g
Carbohydrates	51.4g
Protein	18.9 g
Cholesterol	158 mg
Sodium	1112 mg

* Percent Daily Values are based on a 2,000 calorie diet.

JAPANESE TERIYAKI ZOODLES STIR FRY

Ingredients

- 2 tbsp vegetable oil
- 1 medium onion, thinly sliced
- 2 medium zucchinis, cut into thin strips
- 2 tbsp teriyaki sauce
- 1 tbsp soy sauce
- 1 tbsp toasted sesame seeds
- ground black pepper

Directions

- Place a large pan over medium heat. Heat the oil in it. Add the onion and cook it for 6 min.
- Stir in the zucchini and cook them for 2 min. Add the remaining ingredients and cook them for 6 min. Serve your stir fry right away.
- Enjoy.

Amount per serving (4 total)

Timing Information:

Preparation	10 m
Cooking	10 m
Total Time	20 m

Nutritional Information:

Calories	110 kcal
Fat	8.2 g
Carbohydrates	8.1g
Protein	2.7 g
Cholesterol	0 mg
Sodium	581 mg

* Percent Daily Values are based on a 2,000 calorie diet.

Japanese Condensed Beef Steak Stir Fry

Ingredients

- 2 lb boneless beef sirloin or beef top round steaks (3/4" thick)
- 3 tbsp cornstarch
- 1 (10.5 oz) can Condensed Beef Broth
- 1/2 C. soy sauce
- 2 tbsp sugar
- 2 tbsp vegetable oil
- 4 C. sliced shiitake mushrooms
- 1 head Chinese cabbage (bok choy), thinly sliced
- 2 medium red peppers, cut into 2"-long strips
- 3 stalks celery, sliced
- 2 medium green onions, cut into 2" pieces
- Hot cooked regular long-grain white rice

Directions

- Cut the beef steak into thin strips.
- Get a mixing bowl: Whisk in it the cornstarch, broth, soy and sugar.
- Place a wok or pan over medium heat. Heat in it 1 tbsp of oil. Add half of the beef and cook it for 6 min. Drain it and place it aside. Repeat the process with the rest of the beef.
- Heat the remaining oil in the same pan. Cook in it the mushrooms, cabbage, peppers, celery and green onions for 6 to 8 min. Drain the veggies and place them aside.
- Add the broth mix to the same pan and cook them until they start boiling while stirring all the time. Keep boiling it until the mix becomes thick to make the sauce.
- Toss in back the cooked veggies and beef. Serve your stir fry warm with some white rice.Enjoy.

Amount per serving (8 total)

Timing Information:

Preparation	30 m
Cooking	15 m
Total Time	45 m

Nutritional Information:

Calories	290 kcal
Fat	7.6 g
Carbohydrates	26.4g
Protein	26.4 g
Cholesterol	39 mg
Sodium	1271 mg

* Percent Daily Values are based on a 2,000 calorie diet.

JAPANESE MIRIN CHICKEN SOUP

Ingredients

- 6 C. prepared dashi stock
- 1/4 lb chicken, cut into chunks
- 2 carrots, diced
- 1/3 C. soy sauce
- 3 tbsp mirin
- 1/2 tsp white sugar
- 1/3 tsp salt
- 2 (12 oz) packages firm tofu, cubed

- 1/3 lb shiitake mushrooms, sliced
- 5 ribs and leaves of bok choy, chopped
- 1 (9 oz) package fresh udon noodles
- 4 eggs
- 2 leeks, diced

Directions

- Place a medium pot over medium heat. Stir in it the dashi stock, chicken, carrots, soy sauce, mirin, sugar, and salt. Simmer them for 8 min.
- Stir in the tofu, mushrooms, and bok choy. Cook them for 6 min.
- Add the noodles and cook the soup for 5 min. Stir in the leek with eggs. Simmer the soup for 6 min. Serve it hot.
- Enjoy.

Amount per serving (4 total)

Timing Information:

Preparation	15 m
Cooking	25 m
Total Time	40 m

Nutritional Information:

Calories	548 kcal
Fat	17.2 g
Carbohydrates	53.4g
Protein	42.2 g
Cholesterol	206 mg
Sodium	2491 mg

* Percent Daily Values are based on a 2,000 calorie diet.

Japanese Dashi Omelet

Ingredients

- 4 eggs
- 1/4 C. prepared dashi stock
- 1 tbsp white sugar
- 1 tsp mirin
- 1/2 tsp soy sauce
- 1/2 tsp vegetable oil, or more as needed

Directions

- Get a large mixing bowl: Beat the eggs in it well. Add the dashi stock, sugar, mirin, and soy sauce. Mix them well.
- Place a large skillet over medium heat. Heat the oil in it. Pour enough of the eggs mix to make a thin layer to cover the bottom of the pan.
- Cook it until it becomes firm from the bottom. Roll the omelet and until you reach the side of the skillet and leave it there.
- Grease the skillet again with oil and pour in it another thin layer of the eggs mix. Cook it until it becomes firm and roll it to the side on the first egg roll.
- Repeat the process with the remaining egg mix until it is all used. Serve your omelet warm.
- Enjoy.

Amount per serving (6 total)

Timing Information:

Preparation	15 m
Cooking	10 m
Total Time	25 m

Nutritional Information:

Calories	63 kcal
Fat	3.8 g
Carbohydrates	2.6g
Protein	4.4 g
Cholesterol	124 mg
Sodium	87 mg

* Percent Daily Values are based on a 2,000 calorie diet.

Japanese Chicken Snow Soup

Ingredients

- 3 C. chicken stock
- 1 C. water
- 1 tbsp minced fresh ginger root
- 1 clove garlic, minced
- 2 tbsp soy sauce

- 2 skinless, boneless chicken breast halves - cubed
- 1/4 lb fresh snow peas, trimmed and halved
- 1 carrot, chopped
- 3 fresh mushrooms, sliced
- 2 green onions, chopped

Directions

- Place a medium soup pot over medium heat. Add the chicken stock, water, ginger, garlic, and soy sauce. Cook them until they start simmering.
- Add the chicken and cook the soup again until it starts simmering. Lower the heat and simmer the soup for 17 min.
- Add the carrot with snow peas. Cook the soup for 7 min. Stir in the mushroom and cook the soup for 5 min.
- Add the green onions. Serve your soup warm.
- Enjoy.

Amount per serving (4 total)

Timing Information:

Preparation	15 m
Cooking	25 m
Total Time	40 m

Nutritional Information:

Calories	95 kcal
Fat	1.8 g
Carbohydrates	6.5g
Protein	13.5 g
Cholesterol	30 mg
Sodium	1005 mg

* Percent Daily Values are based on a 2,000 calorie diet.

Japanese Hot Devil's Eggs

Ingredients

- 8 eggs
- 1/3 C. mayonnaise
- 3 tbsp minced green onions
- 2 tsp rice wine vinegar
- 1 1/2 tsp wasabi paste
- coarse salt
- 1/2 C. fresh pea shoots, or as needed
- 16 pickled ginger slices

Directions

- Place a large saucepan over medium heat. Place in it the eggs and cover them water. Cook them until they start boiling.
- Turn off the heat and put on the lid. Allow the eggs to sit for 17 min. Drain the eggs and wash them with some cold water until they cool down.
- Remove the shells of the eggs and slice each one in half. Transfer the egg yolk into a large mixing bowl. Mash them well with a fork or potato masher.
- Add the mayonnaise, green onions, rice wine vinegar, and wasabi paste, a pinch of salt and pepper. Mix them well until they become creamy.
- Place the egg white halves on a serving plate. Pour the egg yolk mix into a piping bag and fill the egg whites with it. Serve your deviled eggs with your favorite toppings.
- Enjoy.

Amount per serving (16 total)

Timing Information:

Preparation	20 m
Cooking	15 m
Total Time	50 m

Nutritional Information:

Calories	74 kcal
Fat	6.1 g
Carbohydrates	1.4g
Protein	<
Cholesterol	3.3 g
Sodium	95 mg

* Percent Daily Values are based on a 2,000 calorie diet.

Japanese Miso Soup

Ingredients

- 3 C. prepared dashi stock
- 1/4 C. sliced shiitake mushrooms
- 1 tbsp miso paste
- 1 tbsp soy sauce
- 1/8 C. cubed soft tofu
- 1 green onion, chopped

Directions

- Place a small saucepan over medium heat. Pour the stock into it and cook it until it starts boiling. Lower the heat.
- Stir in the mushroom and simmer the soup for 4 min.
- Get a small bowl: Add the miso paste and soy sauce. Mix them well. Pour the mix into the soup with tofu and stir them. Cook the soup for 6 min.
- Serve your soup hot with some green onions.
- Enjoy.

Amount per serving (2 total)

Timing Information:

Preparation	10 m
Cooking	10 m
Total Time	20 m

Nutritional Information:

Calories	100 kcal
Fat	3.9 g
Carbohydrates	4.8g
Protein	11 g
Cholesterol	3 mg
Sodium	1326 mg

* Percent Daily Values are based on a 2,000 calorie diet.

Japanese Potato with Homemade Curry

Ingredients

- 2 C. cubed Japanese turnips
- 1 potato, peeled and cubed
- 1 tomato, diced
- 1 C. water
- 1/4 tsp ground turmeric
- Spice Paste:
- 1 tsp canola oil
- 2 dried red chiles
- 2 small Thai green chiles
- 1 (1/2 inch) piece cinnamon stick
- 4 pearl onions
- 2 tbsp unsweetened dried coconut
- 1 tbsp coriander seeds
- 5 cashews
- 2 green cardamom pods
- 2 whole cloves
- 1/2 tsp fennel seeds
- 1/4 tsp cumin seeds
- 2 tbsp chopped cilantro
- 2 tbsp chopped fresh mint
- 1 tsp water, or as needed
- 1 tsp canola oil
- 1/2 tsp fennel seeds
- 1 (1 inch) piece cinnamon stick
- 2 cloves garlic, minced
- 1 (1 inch) piece fresh ginger root, minced
- 4 fresh curry leaves
- 1/4 C. peas
- 1 pinch salt, or to taste

Directions

- Place a small saucepan over medium heat. Stir in it the turnips, potato, and diced tomato, 1 C. water and turmeric. Cook them until they start boiling.
- Lower the heat and cook the soup for 17 min.

- Place a large pan over medium heat. Heat 1 tsp of oil in it.
- Add the red chiles and green chiles, 1/2-inch cinnamon stick, pearl onions, coconut, coriander, cashews, cardamom pods, cloves, 1/2 tsp fennel seeds, and cumin seeds.
- Cook them for 4 min while stirring all the time. Turn off the heat and transfer the mix to a spice grinder.
- Stir in the cilantro, mint, and 1 tsp water. Grind them while adding more water if needed until the mix becomes smooth and like a paste.
- Place a clean pan over medium heat. Heat in it 1 tsp of canola oil. Cook in it 1/2 tsp fennel seeds and 1-inch cinnamon stick for 40 sec.
- Stir in the minced garlic, ginger, and curry leaves. Cook them for 3 min. Stir in the cooked veggies with the spices paste then cook them until they start boiling.
- Stir in more water if the stew is too thick to your liking. Add the green peas with a pinch of salt and pepper.
- Lower the heat and cook the stew for 12 min. Serve it warm.
- Enjoy.

Amount per serving (2 total)

Timing Information:

Preparation	30 m
Cooking	30 m
Total Time	1 h

Nutritional Information:

Calories	297 kcal
Fat	11.6 g
Carbohydrates	45.1g
Protein	8 g
Cholesterol	0 mg
Sodium	236 mg

* Percent Daily Values are based on a 2,000 calorie diet.

JAPANESE HOT SHISO GUACAMOLE

Ingredients

- 2 large avocados - halved, peeled, and pitted
- 1 lime, juiced
- 1 onion, minced
- 2 jalapeno peppers, or to taste, seeded and minced
- 10 shiso leaves, chopped
- 1 tbsp minced fresh ginger root
- 1 tsp wasabi paste
- 1/2 tsp ground white pepper
- 2 drops hot pepper sauce
- 1 tomato, chopped
- salt and black pepper to taste

Directions

- Get a large mixing bowl: Mix in it the avocados, lime juice, onion, jalapeno pepper, shiso leaf, ginger, wasabi paste, white pepper, and hot sauce until it becomes slightly mashed.
- Stir in the tomato with a pinch of salt and pepper. Serve your guacamole.
- Enjoy.

Amount per serving (12 total)

Timing Information:

Preparation	
Cooking	20 m
Total Time	20 m

Nutritional Information:

Calories	90 kcal
Fat	7 g
Carbohydrates	7.5g
Protein	1.4 g
Cholesterol	0 mg
Sodium	15 mg

* Percent Daily Values are based on a 2,000 calorie diet.

WASABI JAPANESE TORTILLAS

Ingredients

- 1/4 C. soy sauce
- 2 tbsp white sugar
- 1 tsp grated fresh ginger
- 1 clove garlic, minced
- 1 lb skinless, boneless chicken breast, cut into strips
- 6 (10 inch) flour tortillas
- 1/4 C. extra-virgin olive oil, divided
- 6 oz shredded pepperjack cheese, divided
- 6 oz grated Parmesan cheese, divided
- 1 habanero pepper, seeded and finely chopped (optional)
- 1 tbsp wasabi paste, divided (optional)

Directions

- Get a large mixing bowl: Mix in it the soy sauce, sugar, ginger, and garlic. Add the chicken strips and stir them.
- Place a piece of plastic wrap on the bowl. Place it in the fridge for 1 h 20 min. Before you do anything preheat the oven to 425 F.
- Drain the chicken strips from the marinade. Lay them in a glass oven dish. Cook them in the oven for 22 min.
- Spread the olive oil on both sides of a tortilla. Place it on a lined up baking sheet and spread 1/3 of the pepperjack cheese on it followed by 1/3 of chicken strips. Place 1/3 of the parmesan cheese followed by 1/3 of the habanero and 1 tsp wasabi paste. Cover another tortilla with some olive oil on both sides and place it on top to make a quesadilla. Repeat the process to make another 2 quesadillas.
- Place a griddle over medium heat and grease it with some oil. Place in it a quesadilla and cook it for 4 min on each side.
- Repeat the process with the remaining 2 quesadillas then serve them warm. Enjoy.

Amount per serving (6 total)

Timing Information:

Preparation	30 m
Cooking	26 m
Total Time	1 h 56 m

Nutritional Information:

Calories	643 kcal
Fat	33.5 g
Carbohydrates	44.9g
Protein	38.2 g
Cholesterol	94 mg
Sodium	1737 mg

* Percent Daily Values are based on a 2,000 calorie diet.

JAPANESE JASMINE NORI BITES

Ingredients

- 2 C. water
- 1 C. jasmine rice
- salt
- 1 sheet nori (dry seaweed), cut into 1-inch strips, or as desired (optional)

Directions

- Prepare the rice according to the directions on the package. Drain it, fluff it and place it aside to lose heat for 12 min.
- Get a small bowl: fill it with water and place it aside. Fill another small bowl with 2 tbsp of salt.
- Wet your hands with the water and rub some salt all over it. Take some rice into your hands and shape them into a triangle. Wrap a strip of nori around the triangle.
- Serve them with your favorite dip.
- Enjoy.

Amount per serving (6 total)

Timing Information:

Preparation	20 m
Cooking	25 m
Total Time	55 m

Nutritional Information:

Calories	114 kcal
Fat	0 g
Carbohydrates	25.6g
Protein	2.2 g
Cholesterol	0 mg
Sodium	28 mg

* Percent Daily Values are based on a 2,000 calorie diet.

Japanese Sesame Wings

Ingredients

- 14 oz chicken wings
- 1 tbsp sake
- 1 tbsp chopped garlic
- 1 1/2 tsp sesame oil
- 1 tsp chopped fresh ginger root
- 1/2 tsp salt
- 1/2 tsp dashi (Japanese seasoning)
- 2 C. vegetable oil for frying
- 3 tbsp cornstarch
- salt and ground black pepper to taste

Directions

- Get a large mixing bowl: Toss in it the chicken wings, sake, garlic, sesame oil, ginger, dashi, and 1/2 tsp salt. Cover the bowl and place it in the fridge for 1 h 30 min.
- Place a saucepan over medium heat. Heat the oil in it until it reaches 350 F.
- Drain the chicken wings from the marinade and dust them with the cornstarch. Deep fry the chicken wings until they become golden brown for 17 min.
- Drain them then season them with some salt and pepper. Serve your chicken wings with your favorite dip.
- Enjoy.

Amount per serving (4 total)

Timing Information:

Preparation	15 m
Cooking	10 m
Total Time	1 h 25 m

Nutritional Information:

Calories	224 kcal
Fat	18.3 g
Carbohydrates	7g
Protein	6.6 g
Cholesterol	20 mg
Sodium	349 mg

* Percent Daily Values are based on a 2,000 calorie diet.

SAVORY AND SWEET OMELET

Ingredients

- 1 tbsp water
- 1 tsp soy sauce, or to taste
- 1/2 tsp white sugar
- 1 egg

Directions

- Get a mixing bowl: Whisk in it the water, soy sauce, and sugar well. Stir in the egg and mix them again.
- Place a large skillet over medium heat. Grease it with a cooking spray. Pour into it the egg mix and spread it in the pan.
- Cook it for 4 min until it becomes golden brown from the sides. Serve it warm.
- Enjoy.

Amount per serving (1 total)

Timing Information:

Preparation	10 m
Cooking	5 m
Total Time	15 m

Nutritional Information:

Calories	82 kcal
Fat	5 g
Carbohydrates	2.9g
Protein	6.6 g
Cholesterol	186 mg
Sodium	369 mg

* Percent Daily Values are based on a 2,000 calorie diet.

TIPSY JAPANESE CRUMBLED BEEF

Ingredients

- 3/4 lb ground beef
- 2 tbsp freshly grated ginger
- 3 tbsp soy sauce
- 3 tbsp sake
- 2 tbsp mirin
- 1 tbsp white sugar, or more to taste

Directions

- Place a large skillet over medium heat and heat it. Add the beef and cook it for 8 min.
- Stir in the remaining ingredients. Cook them until they start boiling. Keep boiling them for 2 min. Serve your crumbled beef warm with some rice.
- Enjoy.

Amount per serving (4 total)

Timing Information:

Preparation	10 m
Cooking	6 m
Total Time	16 m

Nutritional Information:

Calories	232 kcal
Fat	13.2 g
Carbohydrates	7.4g
Protein	14.9 g
Cholesterol	52 mg
Sodium	726 mg

* Percent Daily Values are based on a 2,000 calorie diet.

JAPANESE RICY KETCHUP OMELET

Ingredients

- 1 C. cooked white or brown rice
- 2 thin slices cooked ham, cubed
- 2 tbsp ketchup
- 1 slice processed cheese food (such as Velveeta (R)) (optional)
- 2 eggs
- salt and pepper to taste
- 1 tbsp ketchup
- 1/4 tsp chopped fresh parsley

Directions

- Place a large skillet over medium heat and heat it. Grease it with a cooking spray.
- Add the rice, 2 tbsp ketchup, ham, and cheese. Cook them for 9 min. Transfer the mix to a serving dish and place it aside.
- Get a mixing bowl: Mix in it the eggs and salt and pepper.
- Place a small skillet over medium heat and heat it. Grease it with a cooking spray. Pour in it the beaten egg and cook the omelet until it becomes golden brown from the bottom.
- Serve your omelet over the rice warm.
- Enjoy.

Amount per serving (1 total)

Timing Information:

Preparation	5 m
Cooking	15 m
Total Time	20 m

Nutritional Information:

Calories	521 kcal
Fat	20.2 g
Carbohydrates	59.3g
Protein	26.7 g
Cholesterol	403 mg
Sodium	1300 mg

* Percent Daily Values are based on a 2,000 calorie diet.

Japanese Tofu and Beef Burgers

Ingredients

- 1 (14 oz) package firm tofu
- 1 lb ground beef
- 1/2 C. sliced shiitake mushrooms
- 2 tbsp miso paste
- 1 egg, lightly beaten
- 1 tsp salt
- 1 tsp ground black pepper
- 1/4 tsp ground nutmeg
- 1/4 C. mirin (Japanese sweet wine)
- 2 tbsp soy sauce
- 1 tsp garlic paste
- 1/4 tsp minced fresh ginger root
- 1 tbsp vegetable oil

Directions

- Press the tofu and drain it. Cut it into 1/2 inch dices.
- Get a large mixing bowl: Mix in it the tofu, ground beef, shiitake mushrooms, miso paste, egg, salt, pepper, and nutmeg. Shape the mix into 6 patties.
- Get a small bowl: Mix in it the mirin, soy sauce, garlic paste, and ginger.
- Place a large pan over medium heat. Heat the oil in it. Cook in it the patties for 3 min on each side.
- Lower the heat and put on the lid. Cook the patties for 5 min. Drain them and place them aside.
- Discard the grease from the pan. Add the mirin mix with the burger patties. Cook them on both sides until they become coated with the sauce.
- Serve your burgers with your favorite toppings.
- Enjoy.

Amount per serving (6 total)

Timing Information:

Preparation	25 m
Cooking	20 m
Total Time	45 m

Nutritional Information:

Calories	307 kcal
Fat	18.1 g
Carbohydrates	8.9g
Protein	25.5 g
Cholesterol	77 mg
Sodium	999 mg

* Percent Daily Values are based on a 2,000 calorie diet.

Japanese Grilled Portobello Caps

Ingredients

- 4 Portobello mushroom caps
- 3 tbsp soy sauce
- 2 tbsp sesame oil
- 1 tbsp minced fresh ginger root
- 1 small clove garlic, minced

Directions

- Before you do anything preheat the oven broiler. Place the rack 6 inches away from the heat.
- Clean the mushroom caps and place them on a baking pan with their top down.
- Get a small bowl: Mix in it the soy sauce, sesame oil, ginger, and garlic. Spread the mix over the mushroom caps.
- Place it in the oven and cook it for 12 min. Serve it warm.
- Enjoy.

Amount per serving (2 total)

Timing Information:

Preparation	5 m
Cooking	10 m
Total Time	15 m

Nutritional Information:

Calories	196 kcal
Fat	14.1 g
Carbohydrates	14.2g
Protein	7.3 g
Cholesterol	0 mg
Sodium	1367 mg

* Percent Daily Values are based on a 2,000 calorie diet.

Japanese Sweet and Chili Cucumber Salad

Ingredients

- 2 tbsp white sugar
- 2 tbsp rice vinegar
- 1 tsp Asian (toasted) sesame oil
- 1 tsp chili paste
- salt to taste
- 2 large cucumbers - peeled, seeded, and cut into 1/4-inch slices

Directions

- Get a large mixing bowl: Whisk in it the sugar, rice vinegar, sesame oil, chile paste, and salt.
- Add the cucumber and toss them to coat. Place the salad aside to sit for 35 min. Serve it.
- Enjoy.

Amount per serving (4 total)

Timing Information:

Preparation	
Cooking	15 m
Total Time	45 m

Nutritional Information:

Calories	55 kcal
Fat	1.6 g
Carbohydrates	10.5g
Protein	0.8 g
Cholesterol	0 mg
Sodium	111 mg

* Percent Daily Values are based on a 2,000 calorie diet.

CRUSTED JAPANESE CHICKEN BREASTS

Ingredients

- 4 skinless, boneless chicken breast halves – pound it to 1/2 inch thickness
- salt and pepper to taste
- 2 tbsp all-purpose flour
- 1 egg, beaten
- 1 C. panko bread crumbs
- 1 C. oil for frying, or as needed

Directions

- Sprinkle some salt and pepper over the chicken breasts.
- Place the egg, flour and breadcrumbs in separate shallow bowls. Dip the chicken breasts in the egg, dust them with flour and coat them with the breadcrumbs.
- Place a large frying pan over medium heat. Heat the oil in it until it starts shimmering. Deep dry in it the chicken for 5 min on each side. Serve them warm.
- Enjoy.

Amount per serving (4 total)

Timing Information:

Preparation	10 m
Cooking	10 m
Total Time	20 m

Nutritional Information:

Calories	297 kcal
Fat	11.4 g
Carbohydrates	22.2g
Protein	31.2 g
Cholesterol	118 mg
Sodium	251 mg

* Percent Daily Values are based on a 2,000 calorie diet.

Japanese Sesame Fried Chicken Bites

Ingredients

- 2 eggs, lightly beaten
- 1/2 tsp salt
- 1/2 tsp black pepper
- 1/2 tsp white sugar
- 1 tbsp minced garlic
- 1 tbsp grated fresh ginger root
- 1 tbsp sesame oil
- 1 tbsp soy sauce
- 1/8 tsp chicken bouillon granules
- 1 1/2 lb skinless, boneless chicken breast halves - cut into 1 inch cubes
- 3 tbsp potato starch
- 1 tbsp rice flour
- oil for frying

Directions

- Get a large mixing bowl: Beat in it the eggs, salt, pepper, sugar, garlic, ginger, sesame oil, soy sauce, and bouillon.
- Dip in it the chicken dices. Cover bowl with a plastic wrap and place it in the fridge for 35 min.
- Get a large shallow bowl: Mix in it the potato starch and rice flour. Toss in it the chicken cubes.
- Place a large frying pan over medium heat. Heat the oil in it until it reaches 365 F. Cook in it the chicken cubes until they become golden brown.
- Drain your chicken cubes then serve them warm with your favorite dip.
- Enjoy.

Amount per serving (8 total)

Timing Information:

Preparation	20 m
Cooking	20 m
Total Time	1 h 10 m

Nutritional Information:

Calories	256 kcal
Fat	16.7 g
Carbohydrates	4.8g
Protein	20.9 g
Cholesterol	98 mg
Sodium	327 mg

* Percent Daily Values are based on a 2,000 calorie diet.

JAPANESE BARBECUE BACON PANCAKES

Ingredients

- 12 oz sliced bacon
- 1 1/3 C. water
- 4 eggs
- 3 C. all-purpose flour
- 1 tsp salt
- 1 medium head cabbage, cored and sliced
- 2 tbsp minced pickled ginger
- 1/4 C. tonkatsu sauce or barbeque sauce

Directions

- Place a large pan over medium heat. Cook in it the bacon slices until they become crisp. Drain it and place it aside.
- Get a large mixing bowl: Whisk in it the eggs with water. Add the salt with flour. Mix them well. Stir in the ginger with cabbage.
- Place a large skillet over medium heat then grease it with a cooking spray. Ladle about 1/4 of the batter into the hot skillet. Place 4 crisp bacon slices in the middle of the pancake.
- Cook the pancake for 6 min. Flip it and cook it on the other side until it is done. Repeat the process with the rest of the batter.
- Serve your pancakes with the tonkatsu sauce.
- Enjoy.

Amount per serving (4 total)

Timing Information:

Preparation	15 m
Cooking	30 m
Total Time	45 m

Nutritional Information:

Calories	659 kcal
Fat	19.4 g
Carbohydrates	90.7g
Protein	29.3 g
Cholesterol	217 mg
Sodium	1531 mg

* Percent Daily Values are based on a 2,000 calorie diet.

JAPANESE SWEET CHICKEN STIR FRY

Ingredients

- 1 (3 lb) whole chicken, cut into pieces
- 1 tbsp grated fresh ginger root
- 1 clove garlic, crushed
- 3 tbsp white sugar
- 2/3 C. soy sauce
- 1 tbsp sake
- 1/4 C. mirin
- 2 tbsp cooking oil

Directions

- Clean the chicken and dry it.
- Get a glass oven pan: Mix in it the ginger, garlic, sugar, soy sauce, sake and mirin. Add to it the chicken pieces and stir them to coat.
- Cover the dish with a plastic wrap and place it in the fridge for 2 h to 8 h.
- Place a large skillet over medium heat. Heat the oil in it. Drain the chicken pieces from the marinade and fry them until they become golden brown.
- Drain the chicken pieces and place them aside. Remove the grease from the pan Pour the marinade from the chicken into the skillet with the browned chicken pieces.
- Lower the heat and put on the lid. Cook the marinade for 9 min to make the sauce. Remove the lid and keep cooking them until the chicken is done and the sauce is thick.
- Serve your saucy chicken warm. Enjoy.

Amount per serving (4 total)

Timing Information:

Preparation	20 m
Cooking	20 m
Total Time	1 d 40 m

Nutritional Information:

Calories	587 kcal
Fat	32.5 g
Carbohydrates	18g
Protein	48.7 g
Cholesterol	146 mg
Sodium	2545 mg

* Percent Daily Values are based on a 2,000 calorie diet.

Japanese Sesame Egg Sushi

Ingredients

- 1 C. sushi rice, or Japanese short-grain white rice
- 3 eggs, beaten
- 1/4 tsp salt
- 1 tbsp vegetable oil
- 3 tbsp rice vinegar
- 2 tbsp white sugar
- 1 tsp salt
- 2 tbsp black sesame seeds
- 6 sprigs Italian parsley with long stems

Directions

- Cook the rice according to the directions on the package. Drain and place it aside to lose heat completely.
- Get a mixing bowl: Mix in it the eggs with 1/4 tsp of salt.
- Place a large skillet over medium heat. Grease it with oil and heat it. Spread in it 1/6 of the beaten eggs then cook them for until it is done.
- Flip the egg omelet and cook it for 10 sec. Place it aside. Repeat the process with the rest of the mix to make 6 thin omelet.
- Get a small bowl: Mix in it the vinegar, sugar, and 1 tsp salt. Place it in the microwave and heat for 10 to 15 sec.
- Stir in the sesame seeds with vinegar.
- Place an egg omelet on working surface and place in the center of the edge a spoonful of rice. Roll it to make a square then use the Italian parsley to tie it.
- Serve it with your favorite dip.
- Enjoy.

Amount per serving (6 total)

Timing Information:

Preparation	30 m
Cooking	25 m
Total Time	55 m

Nutritional Information:

Calories	218 kcal
Fat	6.7 g
Carbohydrates	33.2g
Protein	6.7 g
Cholesterol	93 mg
Sodium	535 mg

* Percent Daily Values are based on a 2,000 calorie diet.

Nori Noodles Soup

Ingredients

- 1 (8 oz) package dried soba noodles
- 1 C. prepared dashi stock
- 1/4 C. soy sauce
- 2 tbsp mirin
- 1/4 tsp white sugar
- 2 tbsp sesame seeds
- 1/2 C. chopped green onions
- 1 sheet nori (dried seaweed), cut into thin strips (optional)

Directions

- Cook the noodles according to the directions on the package. Drain it and cool it down with some water.
- Place a small saucepan over medium heat. Stir in it the dashi, soy sauce, mirin, and white sugar. Cook it until it starts boiling.
- Turn off the heat and allow the mix to lose heat for 27 min. Divide the sesame seeds with noodles on serving bowls and pour the stock soup over it.
- Garnish your soup bowls with the nori and green onions.
- Enjoy.

Amount per serving (4 total)

Timing Information:

Preparation	10 m
Cooking	15 m
Total Time	50 m

Nutritional Information:

Calories	257 kcal
Fat	3.1 g
Carbohydrates	48.2g
Protein	11.6 g
Cholesterol	1 mg
Sodium	1445 mg

* Percent Daily Values are based on a 2,000 calorie diet.

VANILLA CRUSTED SHRIMP

Ingredients

- 32 vanilla wafers, crushed
- 1 egg, beaten
- 3/4 C. water
- 1/3 C. apricot nectar
- 2 tsp cornstarch
- 1/4 C. packed brown sugar
- 3 tbsp red wine vinegar
- 1 tbsp ketchup
- 2 C. vegetable oil
- 3/4 lb medium shrimp - peeled and deveined

Directions

- Get a small bowl: Mix in it the vanilla wafers, egg, and water. Place the mix in the fridge for 1 h 30 min.
- Get a small saucepan: Mix in it the nectar with cornstarch. Add the brown sugar, vinegar and ketchup.
- Place the mix over medium heat and cook them while stirring all the time until it becomes thick to make the sauce. Place it aside.
- Heat the oil in a large pot or deep fryer until it reaches 375 F. Coat the shrimp with the egg mix then cook it in the hot oil until it becomes golden brown.
- Drain the shrimp and serve it with the ketchup sauce.
- Enjoy.

Amount per serving (6 total)

Timing Information:

Preparation	5 m
Cooking	10 m
Total Time	2 h 15 m

Nutritional Information:

Calories	920 kcal
Fat	81.4 g
Carbohydrates	35.8g
Protein	14.1 g
Cholesterol	117 mg
Sodium	225 mg

* Percent Daily Values are based on a 2,000 calorie diet.

Jalapenos Frittata

Ingredients

- 2 (3 oz) packages chicken flavored ramen noodles
- 6 eggs
- 2 tsp butter
- 1/2 C. shredded Cheddar cheese

Directions

- Place a small saucepan over medium heat. Fill it with water and bring it to a boil. Cook in it the noodles until it becomes soft.
- Get a mixing bowl: Mix in it the seasoning packet with eggs. Add the noodles and toss them.
- Place a large pan over medium heat. Heat the butter in it until it melts. Cook in it the noodles for 6 min.
- Cut the noodles frittata into 4 pieces and flip them. Sprinkle the cheese on top and cook them for 2 min. Serve your frittata warm.
- Enjoy.

Amount per serving (4 total)

Timing Information:

Preparation	5 m
Cooking	15 m
Total Time	20 m

Nutritional Information:

Calories	339 kcal
Fat	15.7 g
Carbohydrates	28.8g
Protein	20.3 g
Cholesterol	302 mg
Sodium	681 mg

* Percent Daily Values are based on a 2,000 calorie diet.

Japanese Tuna Pyramids Bites

Ingredients

- 1 C. short-grain sushi rice
- 1 1/4 C. water
- 1 pinch salt (optional)
- 1 (5 oz) can tuna, drained
- 2 tbsp mayonnaise, or to taste
- ground black pepper (optional)
- 1 sheet nori, cut into 1-inch strips, or desired width

Directions

- Clean the rice well with some water.
- Place a medium saucepan over medium heat. Pour into it 1 1/4 C. of water. Add the rice with a pinch of salt. Cook it until it starts boiling.
- Lower the heat and put on the lid. Cook the rice for 22 min. Place the rice aside with the cover on for 12 min.
- Transfer the rice to a mixing bowl and place it aside to lose heat completely for 17 min.
- Get a mixing bowl: Mix in it the tuna, mayonnaise, a pinch of salt and pepper.
- Lay 10 inches piece of a plastic wrap on a working surface. Place in the middle of it 1/2 of rice. Create a small well in it and place in it 1 tsp of the tuna mix.
- Cover it with another 1/2 C. of rice. Fold the plastic wrap over the rice mix to cover it. Shape the mix into a small pyramid then remove the plastic wrap.
- Wrap a nori strip around the rice pyramid gently. Repeat the process with the remaining mix then serve them with your favorite dip. Enjoy.

Amount per serving (3 total)

Timing Information:

Preparation	30 m
Cooking	20 m
Total Time	1 h 15 m

Nutritional Information:

Calories	355 kcal
Fat	8 g
Carbohydrates	53.3g
Protein	15.2 g
Cholesterol	16 mg
Sodium	129 mg

* Percent Daily Values are based on a 2,000 calorie diet.

Japanese Grilled Tuna Salad

Ingredients

- 2 tbsp olive oil
- 1 1/2 tsp lime juice
- 1 1/2 tsp chopped fresh cilantro
- 1/2 tsp garlic, minced
- 1 tsp chopped fresh mint
- 1/2 tsp lemon juice
- 1/8 tsp salt
- 1 1/2 C. mixed baby salad greens
- 1/2 C. torn romaine lettuce

- 2 tbsp diced mango
- 1 1/2 tsp roasted peanuts
- 4 slices cucumber, quartered
- 2 tbsp crisp chow mein noodles
- 1 (3 oz) fresh ahi (yellowfin) tuna steak
- 1 pinch salt and ground black pepper to taste
- 1/4 avocado, sliced

Directions

- Get a small bowl: Mix in it the olive oil, lime juice, cilantro, garlic, mint, lemon juice, and salt to make the salad dressing. Place it in the fridge for 1 h 30 min to 8 h.
- Before you do anything preheat the grill and grease it.
- Get a large serving bowl: Stir in it the salad greens, romaine lettuce, mango, peanuts, cucumber, and chow mein noodles.
- Season the tuna steaks with some salt and pepper. Cook it on the grill for 2 to 4 min on each side.
- Slice the tuna and place it over the salad. Drizzle the dressing on top then serve your salad.
- Enjoy.

Amount per serving (2 total)

Timing Information:

Preparation	30 m
Cooking	5 m
Total Time	1 h 35 m

Nutritional Information:

Calories	252 kcal
Fat	19.3 g
Carbohydrates	9.3g
Protein	12.4 g
Cholesterol	19 mg
Sodium	207 mg

* Percent Daily Values are based on a 2,000 calorie diet.

NOODLES CURRY SOUP

Ingredients

- 3 carrots, cut into bite-size pieces
- 1 small onion, cut into bite-size pieces
- 3 tbsp water
- 1/4 C. vegetable oil
- 1/2 C. all-purpose flour
- 2 tbsp all-purpose flour
- 2 tbsp red curry powder
- 5 C. hot vegetable stock
- 1/4 C. soy sauce
- 2 tsp maple syrup
- 8 oz udon noodles, or more to taste

Directions

- Get a microwave proof bowl: Stir in it the water with carrot and onion. put on the lid and cook them on high for 4 min 30 sec.
- Place a soup pot over medium heat. Heat the oil in it. Add to it 1/2 C. plus 2 tbsp flour and mix them to make a paste.
- Add the curry with hot stock and cook them for 4 min while mixing all the time. Add the cooked onion and carrot with soy sauce, and maple syrup.
- Cook the noodles according to the directions on the package until it becomes soft.
- Cook the soup until it starts boiling. Stir in the noodles and serve your soup hot.
- Enjoy.

Amount per serving (4 total)

Timing Information:

Preparation	15 m
Cooking	25 m
Total Time	40 m

Nutritional Information:

Calories	442 kcal
Fat	15.8 g
Carbohydrates	65.2g
Protein	9.2 g
Cholesterol	0 mg
Sodium	1854 mg

* Percent Daily Values are based on a 2,000 calorie diet.

JAPANESE BONITO TOFU SOUP

Ingredients

- 4 C. water
- 1/2 C. bonito flakes
- 1 (4 inch) piece dashi kombu
- 1/2 (12 oz) package tofu, cut into chunks
- 1 tsp dried wakame
- 3 tbsp miso paste
- 1/4 C. chopped green onions

Directions

- Pour the water in a large pot and bring it to a boil over low heat. Add the kombu and bring it to a simmer.
- Add the bonito. Turn off the heat and allow the mix to sit for 6 min to make the stock. Strain the stock and place it aside.
- Pour 3 1/2 C. of the stock in a soup pot and cook it over medium heat until it heated. Add the tofu and wakame.
- Ladles 1 C. of the stock into a mixing bowl. Add the miso paste and mix them well. Pour the mix back into the pot with remaining 1/2 C. of stock. Serve your soup warm with green onions.
- Enjoy.

Amount per serving (4 total)

Timing Information:

Preparation	15 m
Cooking	15 m
Total Time	30 m

Nutritional Information:

Calories	65 kcal
Fat	2.8 g
Carbohydrates	4.9g
Protein	6.2 g
Cholesterol	0 mg
Sodium	511 mg

* Percent Daily Values are based on a 2,000 calorie diet.

Hamburger Bento Soup

Ingredients

- 1 tbsp cooking oil
- 1 onion, diced
- 4 cloves garlic, minced
- 1 large tomato, diced
- 1 pound ground beef
- 4 cups water
- 1 large potato, diced
- 2 tbsps beef bouillon
- 2 tbsps fish sauce
- salt and pepper to taste

Directions

- Cook onions and garlic in hot oil over medium heat until tender add tomatoes and cook for another 3 minutes.
- Now add ground beef and cook for about 5 more minutes or until the color has turned brown.
- Add potato, fish sauce, pepper, beef bouillon, water and some salt into the pan and cook at low heat for 30 minutes while stirring regularly.
- Serve.

Amount per serving: 6

Timing Information:

Preparation	Cooking	Total Time
20 mins	45 mins	1 hr 5 mins

Nutritional Information:

Calories	233 kcal
Carbohydrates	16.9 g
Cholesterol	46 mg
Fat	11.5 g
Fiber	2.4 g
Protein	15.4 g
Sodium	862 mg

* Percent Daily Values are based on a 2,000 calorie diet.

JAPANESE TILAPIA

Ingredients
- 1/2 pound tilapia fillets, cut into chunks
- 1 small head bok choy, chopped
- 2 medium tomatoes, cut into chunks
- 1 cup thinly sliced daikon radish
- 1/4 cup tamarind paste
- 3 cups water
- 2 dried red chile peppers(optional)

Directions
- Combine tilapia, radish, tomatoes, mixture of tamarind paste and water, chili peppers and bok choy.
- Bring the mixture to boil and cook for 5 minutes to get fish tender.
- Serve in appropriate bowls.

Amount per serving: 10

Timing Information:

Preparation	Cooking	Total Time
5 mins	10 mins	15 mins

Nutritional Information:

Calories	112 kcal
Carbohydrates	13.4 g
Cholesterol	21 mg
Fat	1 g
Fiber	2.1 g
Protein	13.1 g
Sodium	63 mg

* Percent Daily Values are based on a 2,000 calorie diet.

BEEF BASED VEGGIE SOUP

Ingredients

- 2 tbsps canola oil
- 1 large onion, chopped
- 2 cloves garlic, chopped
- 1 pound beef stew meat, cut into 1 inch cubes
- 1 quart water
- 2 large tomatoes, diced
- 1/2 pound fresh green beans, rinsed and trimmed
- 1/2 medium head bok choy, cut into 1 1/2 inch strips
- 1 head fresh broccoli, cut into bite size pieces
- 1 (1.41 ounce) package tamarind soup base

Directions

- Cook onion and garlic in hot oil and then add beef to get it brown.
- Now add some water and bring it to a boil.
- Turn the heat down to medium and cook for 30 minutes.
- Cook for another 10 minutes after adding tomatoes and green beans.
- Now add tamarind soup mix, bok choy and some broccoli into the mix and cook for 10 more minutes to get everything tender.

Amount per serving: 6

Timing Information:

Preparation	Cooking	Total Time
15 mins	45 mins	1 hr

Nutritional Information:

Calories	304 kcal
Carbohydrates	15 g
Cholesterol	51 mg
Fat	19.7 g
Fiber	4.5 g
Protein	17.8 g
Sodium	1405 mg

* Percent Daily Values are based on a 2,000 calorie diet.

Printed in Poland
by Amazon Fulfillment
Poland Sp. z o.o., Wrocław